knitting

Baubles, scarves, cushions
and more to knit and crochet

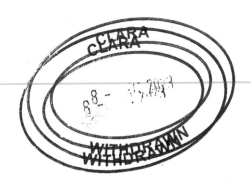

knitting

Baubles, scarves, cushions
and more to knit and crochet

Hikaru Noguchi
Photography by **Hiroko Mori and Koji Udo**
Styling by **Sonia Lucano**

MURDOCH BOOKS

contents

Class: 746.432
Acc: 10/9/61
Inv: 10/329

technical guide

I love needlework, in all its forms. Over the years I have, by turns, practised knitting, crochet, embroidery, appliqué, patchwork and weaving. Using a variety of techniques, often within the same piece, generally leads me to take a simple approach. The elementary techniques used to create most of the patterns presented in this book will allow beginners to achieve satisfactory results and will delight more experienced knitters and crocheters, who will appreciate their simplicity and will no doubt be amazed at the great results they produce.

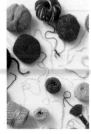

Knitting

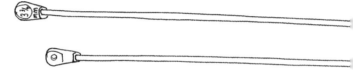

Casting on

FIRST METHOD

1 – Make a first knotted loop and slip it onto a needle.

2 – Hold the needle in one hand, make a loop of yarn with the other hand and slip it over the needle. Continue in this way until you have the required number of stitches.

When you make the loops, always pull on the yarn in the same way so that your stitches are even.

SECOND METHOD

1 – Wrap the wool around your thumb, keeping a length of wool at least three times as wide as the finished piece.

2 – With the other hand, push a needle into the loop of yarn on your thumb, wrap the yarn from the ball around the needle and draw the needle and thread through the loop.

3 – Allow the starting loop to drop off your thumb and pull on it slightly to tighten the stitch on the needle.

Make sure you keep the same tension for all of the stitches.

Casting off

1 – Work two stitches, then insert the left needle into the first stitch made, lift it over the second and let it drop.

2 – Work the next stitch, lift the first stitch on the right needle over the second and let it drop. Repeat as many times as you have stitches to cast off.

3 – When only one stitch is left, cut the thread, open up the stitch to make it bigger, then thread the yarn through the stitch and pull on it to fasten off the work.

continued >>>

Knit stitch

1 – With the yarn at the back, insert the right needle into the front of the first stitch on the left needle.

2 – Wrap the yarn around the right needle, from back to front, then draw the tip of the needle and the loop on it through the stitch, in front of the left needle, so that a new stitch is created, then slip the stitch off the left needle.

Purl stitch

1 – With the yarn at the front, insert the right needle into the first stitch on the left needle, from right to left.

2 – Loop the yarn anti-clockwise around the right needle.

3 – Draw the tip of the right needle and the thread through the base stitch so that a new loop is created and slip the stitch off the left needle.

Single rib stitch

Cast on an even number of stitches. Work one knit stitch and one purl stitch, and repeat these two stitches to the end of the row.

Work all of the rows in the same way.

Garter stitch

Garter stitch is made by working all rows in knit.

Stocking stitch

Work a row entirely in knit and the following row entirely in purl. Keep repeating these two rows. For reverse stocking stitch, begin with the purl row, then the knit.

Moss stitch

Cast on an even number of stitches. Work one knit, one purl, and repeat these two stitches to the end of the row.

The next row, work one purl, one knit and repeat these two stitches to the end of the row.

Keep repeating these two rows.

Decreasing

There are several ways to decrease by a stitch.

Working two knit stitches together: insert the right needle knitwise into the second and first stitch on the left needle and knit them together.

Working two purl stitches together: insert the right needle purlwise into the first two stitches on the left needle, and purl them together.

Slip stitch decrease: insert the right needle into the first stitch on the left needle and slip it onto the right needle without working it. Work the next stitch, then insert the left needle into the slipped stitch and lift it over the worked stitch.

Working two twisted knit stitches together: insert the right needle into the middle of the first stitch, then the second, and knit the two stitches together.

Increasing

In knit: insert the needle into the stitch on the left needle and work a knit stitch without slipping it off the left needle. Then insert the needle into the stitch as if to work a purl stitch, work it and slip the stitch off the left needle.

In purl: proceed in the same way as for a knit stitch increase, this time first working the purl stitch then the knit stitch.

Crochet

Foundation chain

1 – Make a loop in the yarn, insert the hook through the loop, catch the yarn with the hook and draw through to make a slip knot.

2 – Wrap the yarn around the hook (shortened to 'yarn over hook'), and draw a loop through the slip knot to make a chain stitch. For the following chain stitches, wrap the yarn over the hook and draw it through the stitch. Chain stitches are used to make foundation chains, which form the basis of crochet.

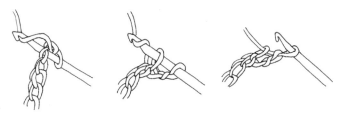

Double crochet

1 – Make a foundation chain, then insert the hook into the second stitch from the hook, yarn over hook (wrap the yarn around the hook) and draw the yarn through to make a loop. You now have two loops on the hook.

2 – Yarn over hook again and draw the yarn through the two loops to make a loop.

Treble crochet

1 – Make a foundation chain, then yarn over hook, count three stitches from the stitch on the hook and insert the hook into this third stitch.

2 – Yarn over hook and draw through the yarn through to make a loop. You now have two loops on the hook.

3 – Yarn over hook again and draw the thread through the first two crochet loops. There are now two loops left on the hook.

4 – Yarn over hook again and draw the thread through the two loops to make one loop.

Crocheting in the round

1 – Make a foundation chain.

2 – Insert the hook into the first chain, yarn over hook (wrap the yarn around the hook) and draw it through the two chain stitches (the first and last stitches of the foundation chain): this is called making a slip stitch.

Half treble crochet

1 – Make a foundation chain, then yarn over hook, count three chains from the chain on the hook, and insert the hook into this chain.

2 – Yarn over hook (wrap the yarn around the hook) and draw the yarn through the first loop. You now have three loops on the hook.

3 – Yarn over hook again and draw the yarn through the three loops. There is one loop left on the hook.

Double treble

1 – Make a foundation chain. Wrap the yarn over the hook twice, count five chains from the chain on the hook and insert the hook into this chain.

2 – Yarn over hook and draw the yarn through one loop. You should have four loops on the hook.

3 – Yarn over hook and draw the yarn through two loops. There are three loops left on the hook.

4 – Yarn over hook and draw the yarn through two loops. There are two loops left on the hook.

5 – Yarn over hook and draw the yarn through the last two loops. There is one loop left on the hook.

Embroidery

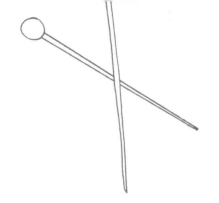

Running stitch

1 – Bring the needle out on the right side of the fabric, reinsert it a little further to the left, bring the needle back out the right side and pull gently on the thread so that you make a small straight stitch.

2 – Insert the needle back into the fabric to make a stitch the same length as the first, and repeat these two steps as many times as required. The stitches and the spaces between the stitches should be the same length.

Chain stitch

1 – Bring the needle out on the right side of the fabric and reinsert it into the same hole to form a loop, without pulling the thread entirely through.

2 – Bring the needle out again a little further along inside the loop, the tip of the needle passing over the top of the thread.

3 – Pull the thread to flatten the loop against the fabric and proceed in the same way to create a second loop that overlaps the first one.

4 – Repeat this process to make a row of loops.

Herringbone stitch

1 – Bring the needle out on the right side of the fabric, reinsert it on the top right-hand side and bring the needle out again a little to the left. Pull the thread to make a large diagonal stitch on the fabric.

2 – Insert the needle at the bottom and bring it out again to the left. Pull on the thread to make another large diagonal stitch. Continue in the same way, making regularly spaced diagonal stitches of the same length. The entry and exit points of the thread must follow two parallel lines.

Stem stitch

1 – Bring the needle out on the right side of the fabric, reinsert it a little further to the right to make a large straight stitch. Bring it out again just above the middle point of the first stitch and reinsert it further to the right.

2 – Repeat step 1 as many times as required, always making stitches of the same length and keeping the thread below the needle.

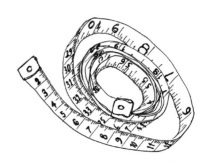

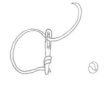

French knot

1 – Bring the needle out on the right side of the fabric, pull the thread through and hold it flat against the fabric with a finger.

2 – Wrap the thread several times around the point of the needle and reinsert it right beside the exit point of the thread.

3 – Slide the loops of thread along the needle as close to the fabric as possible, guiding the thread with a finger, bring the needle out completely on the wrong side and pull the thread to make a knot on the right side.

Blanket stitch

1 – Bring the needle out on the right side of the work, reinsert it on the top right-hand side and bring the needle back out below, further to the right, but at the same level as the exit point, keeping the thread under the needle point.

2 – Pull the thread to flatten the stitch against the fabric, then insert the needle on the top right-hand side and bring it out again below, with the needle on top of the thread. Continue, making stitches of the same height.

Lazy Daisy stitch

1 – Bring the needle out on the right side of the fabric, make a loop with the thread against the fabric, and reinsert the needle back into the same hole.

2 – Bring the needle out inside the loop, pull the thread carefully to properly flatten the loop against the fabric and make a small straight stitch to hold the loop on the fabric.

Appliqué

This technique consists in sewing one piece of fabric onto another one, for decorative purposes. You can do this by sewing running stitch all around the edge of the shape being appliquéd, using a thread of the same colour or a contrasting thread to create a visual effect.

You can also attach the piece of appliqué using small blind running stitches all around the edge. When making these stitches, insert the needle into the background fabric then into the wrong side of the appliqué piece, as for a hem.

How to customise your materials

There is such a variety of fabrics and yarns available in stores that it is sometimes difficult to choose the material and colour that's best suited to a particular pattern. I always start with good-quality raw materials (merino wool, lambswool, angora, mohair, tweed yarn, cotton velvet, woollen felt or flannel), which I customise by dyeing, felting or combining them in original ways. You can easily do the same. Examine your materials carefully and ask yourself how they can be transformed so that they are turned to their best advantage.

In our completely standardised society, objects that are unique are increasingly prized. What does it matter if your jumper isn't knitted perfectly? On the contrary, it's this handmade look that gives it all its charm... and character besides! This artisanal quality is much more precious than the technical perfection produced by a machine.

The simple techniques that follow will help you personalise your materials.

Dyeing

Despite the vast choice of threads and fabrics available in stores, I rarely find the exact shade I want to use. In any case, pieces created using home-dyed products are always more original. That's why I always try to include yarns and/or fabrics I have dyed myself in my pieces.

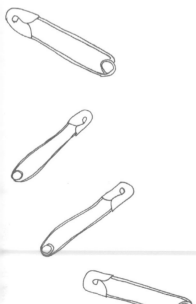

Natural dyes

Working in needlework is a bit like cooking! You can cook dried pasta and serve it with a bought sauce, but it is much less fun and allows for much less variety than making fresh pasta and cooking a home-made sauce!

If you're not afraid to experiment and want to create unique pieces, you can dye your threads and fabric with natural products that you no doubt already have in your cupboard! Red wine gives you a red that borders on pink, strong tea a light brown. Boiling fibres with spinach leaves makes them green; boiling them with onion skins gives them a pale yellow tint. If you would rather limit the amount of experimentation, you can also use a ready-made dye. This type of product offers a vast range of colours and what's more, is simple to use because you just need to follow the manufacturer's instructions to the letter!

Different dyes for different materials

Before beginning, you need to understand that the same dye will produce a different result depending on the material used. This is why you can get two different shades of the same colour if you dye cotton or wool using the same product. Synthetic fabrics are almost always more difficult to dye than those made from natural fibres and, depending on the dye, you sometimes need to fix the colour by soaking the article in water mixed with salt or vinegar. Before buying a ready-made dye, check what materials it is intended for.

Dosage and storage

A packet of dye can contain enough product to dye a few T-shirts or a sheet. You won't need the same amount of dye to colour a skein of embroidery thread, a small knit or 2 m of ribbon. Take out the amount you need with a teaspoon and keep the rest away from humidity, in a small plastic container like a film or bead container.

Don't forget that dyeing is not only for white materials. If you need green wool and you can't find the shade of green that you're looking for, buy pale green wool and dye it with some yellow, khaki or brown to obtain the colour you need.

Precautions for use

When handling dye, always wear old clothes; put on a plastic apron to avoid staining them and rubber gloves to protect your nails!

Assemble everything you will need before beginning. A large jam jar is perfect for dyeing a small length of thread. On the other hand, if you are dyeing large quantities of materials, you might need a large mixing bowl, a stock-pot or even a bucket.

continued >>>

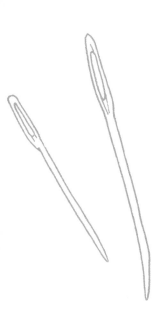
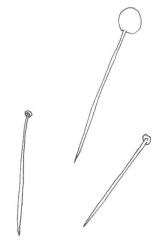

How to dye a small quantity of thread or fabric easily

Use the following method for dyeing embroidery thread or a small piece of knitting or fabric.

1 – Use hot water to wet the material thoroughly.

2 – Put on a plastic apron and rubber gloves. Pour enough very hot water into a second container (to contain the dye, for example a large jam jar) so that you can completely submerge the material; add a teaspoon of salt and a teaspoon of powdered dye and `mix well.

3 – If necessary, add hot water and mix again, then slip the material into the jar. If the jar has a lid, seal it and shake well. If not, stir carefully to thoroughly impregnate the fibres (making sure not to splash yourself with scalding dye!).

4 – Allow to rest for 15 minutes, then remove the material with a pair of pliers or tongs and rinse carefully in hot water. If the resulting colour is too pale, repeat steps 2 and 3, using more dye.

5 – Allow to dry completely then steam-iron the material.

Always do a test with 50 cm thread or a small piece of fabric before dyeing larger quantities.

Warning! The fibres in wool shorten when immersed in hot water; they increase in volume and change texture slightly. If you think these changes might spoil your piece, do a test on a small quantity before dyeing all the material needed to make it.

To dye a large quantity of thread or fabric, use a large container and heat the water in a microwave oven, being very careful not to scald yourself.

Don't be surprised if you are not able to recreate a colour. Even professional dyers never produce exactly the same shade twice. (This is why the labels of balls of yarn and hanks of thread show a dye lot number.)

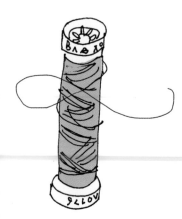

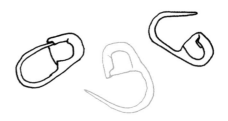

Felt and felting

Felts of various thickness and composition are fabrics obtained by matting together hairs or threads. Easy to cut and sew, they are highly recommended for beginner sewers. They can be made from wool, synthetic fibres or a mixture of materials. Some hat-makers even sell wool and angora felts. The higher the wool content of the felt, the finer its colour and texture... and the more expensive it is!

If you don't find any felt in the colour you want, simply dye a differently-coloured piece. To dye felt successfully, choose a pure-wool material or one with a high wool content and proceed as directed previously. Don't forget that materials that contain a lot of wool may shrink during the process.

If you wish, you can also make your own felt, like the Tibetans! There are different methods for doing this, the simplest being the following.

How to make felt with a washing machine

The technique suggested here amounts to deliberately felting a piece of wool by washing it in the machine (which you sometimes do by accident)!

Each filament of wool is covered in miniscule scales. When wool is soaked in a liquid that is higher than 40°C, its scales open out and hook up with each other in an irreversible fashion. The fabric shrinks during this process and using soap speeds the process up.

Buy a woollen jumper, scarf, jacket or piece of material from a flea-market or garage sale and wash it in the machine at 40°C, with laundry detergent and fabric softener. Let it dry then gently steam-iron with a pressing cloth. Voilà! You've just made felt!

When they are felted, design motifs often lose their sharpness and colours fade, but that is part of the charm of felting. If you steam felt over a boiling kettle, you will obtain a soft and malleable fabric. On the other hand, if the iron comes in contact with the fabric, it will become smooth and stiff. Don't hesitate to conduct multiple experiments to see which effect you prefer.

little accessories

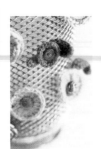

Roll-up mohair brooch

This brooch is made by taking advantage of the natural tendency of stocking stitch to roll up on itself. Make it using leftover yarn to match an item of clothing or bag you have made.

MATERIALS AND TOOLS

5 mm needles
2.5 mm crochet hook
Yarn A: 10 g burgundy-red mohair
Yarn B: 10 g green mohair
Yarn C: 5 g salmon-pink mohair
45 mother-of-pearl beads, 2 mm diameter
Fine needle with a large eye for threading the beads
Safety pin

SIZE

Approximately 10 cm diameter

Construction

With yarn A, cast on 45 sts (approx. 20 cm wide) and work 16 rows in stocking stitch, or until the height measures approx. 4.5 cm (see diagram 1).

With yarn B, cast on 45 sts (approx. 20 cm wide) and work 20 rows, or approx. 8 cm.

Thread the beads on yarn C, then, using the crochet hook, make a 24ch foundation chain. Make 1 row in dtr. Next row, make 1ch, *3dtr, 9ch, incorporating 1 bead in each ch, rep from * to end of row (see diagram 2).

Roll up the beaded strip and sew it together with the salmon-pink yarn.

Thread a drawstring of red yarn through the starting row of the red knitted strip and green yarn through the starting row of the green knitted strip and gather up the two pieces. Join the 3 pieces together, with the wrong side of the stocking stitch facing outwards.

TO FINISH

Sew the pin to the back of the flower.

○ ch
 dtr
○ bead

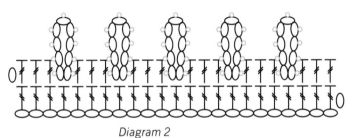

Diagram 2

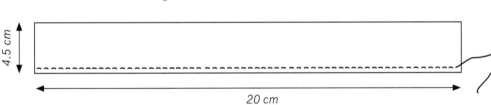

4.5 cm

20 cm

Diagram 1

Mohair brooch

This fluffy flower doesn't require a lot of yarn. You can make it using leftovers, swapping what's left of your balls of wool with friends, or using laine Colbert tapestry wool bought especially to make it.

MATERIALS AND TOOLS

2.5 mm and 3.5 mm crochet hooks
Yarn A: Approx. 10 g yellow mohair
Yarn B: Approx. 10 g brown mohair
16 mother-of-pearl beads, 2 mm diameter
Safety pin

SIZE

9 cm diameter plus fringe
approx. 10 cm long

Construction

With yarn A, make a 52ch foundation chain.
Proceed as per the diagram, beginning with yarn A and finishing with yarn B.
Fasten off.
Thread the beads onto yarn A and make a picot edging decorated with beads along the starting row, proceeding as follows:
Row 1: Work ch st all along the edge, close the round with 1ss.
Row 2: 3dc, *3ch taking 1 bead into the work, 1ss into the base stitch of the picot, 3dc, rep from * to the end of the work. Fasten off.

With yarn A, thread some yarn as a drawstring between the yellow and brown strips and pull to gather the work.
Make a circle and sew a pin to the back of the work.
Thread more beads onto the yarn, make a two-colour fringe and attach it to the back of the brooch.

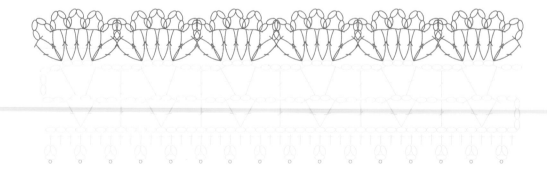

Circular brooches

Make little multicoloured circles with your leftover yarn and use them to decorate your outfits and accessories, but also your furniture or any other sort of objects.

MATERIALS AND TOOLS

3 mm or 3.5 mm crochet hook
Leftover yarn, medium-weight
Old button
Safety pin

SIZE

Variable, depending on the thickness of the yarn and the size of the crochet hook.

Construction

Make 10ch foundation chain and crochet as per the brooch diagram. Attach a button to the centre of the circle and sew a safety pin to the back. Attach the circle to the object to be decorated. If you like, follow the backing diagram using green yarn, or another colour, and sew the backing to the back of the brooch before attaching the safety pin.

Brooch diagram

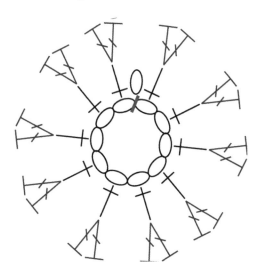

Backing diagram

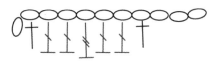

∕ ss
◦ ch
┼ dc
T̄ tr
T̄̄ dtr

Floral brooch

MATERIALS AND TOOLS

3.5 mm crochet hook

Medium-weight white, yellow, green, peach and dusty pink yarn, 5 g of each colour

Leftover bulky slub yarn

Safety pin

SIZE

Stem: 15 cm

Petal: length 8 cm

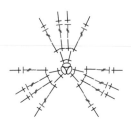

○ ch

⊥ dc

Ŧ dtr

Construction

Make 5 flowers as follows:

Make 3ch foundation chain and join with 1ss.

Round 1: 2dc into each ch (6dc).

Round 2: 2dc into each dc (12dc).

Round 3: 1dtr into each ch.

Round 4: 1dc into each ch.

Make 2 stems with 1 leaf and 3 stems with 2 leaves.

To make 1 stem, make 34ch foundation chain, miss 1ch, 2dc, 2tr, 2dtr, 2tr, 2dc, dc to end of row.

Join the leaves to the stems using 1ss, following the diagrams.

Cut 2 lengths of thread of approx. 20 cm and use them to tie the flower stems together.

Attach a safety pin to the back of the bouquet so that it can be fastened like a brooch.

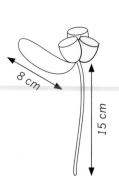

8 cm

15 cm

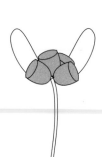

Felted wool brooches

What a wonderful way of using woollen articles that have been felted in the wash. Each brooch will be unique because you can never make two that are exactly identical.

MATERIALS AND TOOLS

Old pure-wool scarf or jumper

Woollen flannel

Woollen fabric

Lightweight felt remnant 8 x 2.5 cm

Buttons

Safety pin

Embroidery needle

Yellow embroidery cotton

SIZE

Approx. 13 cm diameter

Construction

FLOWER 1

Wash the woollen articles at 40°C, allow them to dry then steam-iron them.

Cut out 7 petals in one colour out of the felted wool, 3 in another colour and 2 strips measuring approx. 1 x 20 cm.

Wash the pieces again at 30°C, allow them to dry then iron them with a steam iron.

Arrange the 7 petals in the same colour in a circle, place the 3 other petals on top and sew them all together. Arrange the thin strips in the middle of the flower and fasten them in place with a button. Sew a pin to the back of the piece.

FLOWER 2

Wash the articles as indicated above for flower 1, then cut out 7 petals in one colour and 5 in another.

Using the same template, cut 6 shapes out of the woollen flannel which are a little larger than a petal. Sew the pieces two by two along the curved edge then turn them inside-out.

Cut the felt as per the diagram.

Arrange the felt in a circle, place the petals all around and sew it all together.
Keep the petals in place by making French knots, starting from the centre and going towards the edges of the flower.

FLOWER 3

Wash the articles as previously indicated, then cut out 7 dark-coloured petals and 3 patterned petals. Use the template to cut out some slightly larger petals in a blue fabric and fray their edges using a needle.

Arrange the petals in a circle, placing the blue ones underneath and the patterned ones on top. Sew the petals together and fasten a coloured button in the middle. Add some yellow French knots, starting from the middle of the flower, to imitate pollen.

Crocheted plant necklace

These stylised leaves are quick to crochet. Choose a yarn in a contrasting colour to a plain outfit or make a green necklace, decorated with red berries, to wear at Christmas time.

MATERIALS AND TOOLS

3 mm crochet hook

Yarn A: 10 g medium-weight beige yarn

Yarn B: 10 g medium-weight green yarn

Yarn C: 10 g silver lurex

1 button, 22 mm diameter

LENGTH

Approx. 1 m

Construction

Following the diagrams, crochet the 1st repeated sequence 11 times in the beige yarn and the green yarn and the next sequence 10 times in the lurex. Fasten off. Join the ends of the three pieces together, attaching a button to one of the ends and making a chain loop at the other end. Fasten the necklace and put it on!

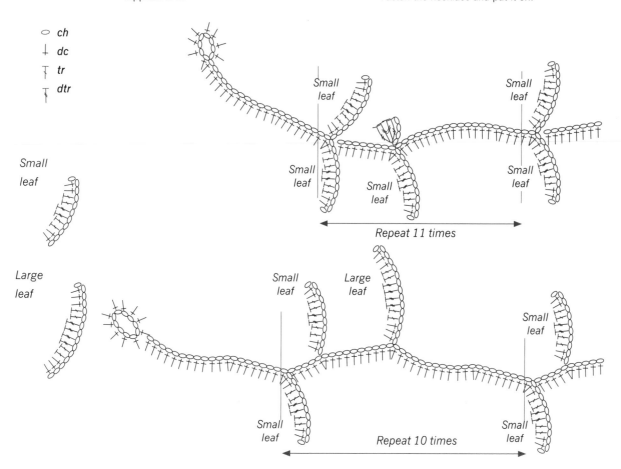

scarves, gloves and beanies

Moss stitch scarf and mittens

These striped mittens and matching fringed scarf are both simple and quick to knit. Choose a soft and natural yarn so that they keep you nice and warm and don't itch.

MATERIALS AND TOOLS

4 mm and 4.5 mm needles
4 mm crochet hook
Yarn A: 125 g medium-weight pale blue heathered yarn
Yarn B: 125 g medium-weight chocolate brown heathered yarn
30 g chunky brown yarn for the fringe
Tapestry needle

TENSION

21 sts and 32 rows = 10 x 10 cm

SIZE

Scarf: 18 x 170 cm
Mittens: 15 x 8 cm

Construction

SCARF

With yarn A and the 4.5 mm needles, cast on 36 st.
Work 10 rows in moss stitch.
Using yarn B, work 10 more rows as per the diagram, running yarn A along the edge of the work.
Repeat these stripes over 530 rows.
Cast off.

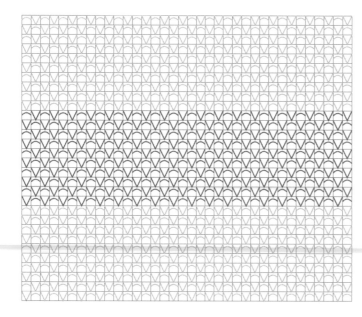

∨   *knit*

⌒   *purl*

continued >>>

FRINGE

Using the chunky yarn and crochet hook, make a fringe by attaching a length of yarn to each of the stitches in the first and last rows of the scarf. For each strand in the fringe: cut a length of yarn measuring approx. 40 cm, fold it in two, draw the loop end through the stitch using the crochet hook, thread the ends of the piece of yarn through the loop and pull. Repeat for the following stitches to make a thick fringe.

STRIPED MITTENS

Using the 4 mm needles and yarn B, cast on 40 sts.
Work 4 rows in single rib then change yarn.
Work 6 cm in single rib, changing the yarn every 4 rows.
Continue with the 4.5 mm needles and work 5 cm in moss stitch, changing yarn every 4 rows.
For the thumb opening, work 22 sts, cast off 6 sts and work the remaining 12 sts in the row.
Turn the work around, work 12 sts, cast on 6 sts and work the remaining 22 sts in the row.
Continue for 3 cm in moss stitch.
Continue for 3 cm in single rib.
Cast off the sts knitwise or purlwise, as they present themselves.
Repeat for the 2nd mitten, reversing the position of the thumb-opening (12 sts, cast off 6 sts and work the remaining 22 sts in the row, then next row: 22 sts, cast on 6 sts and work the remaining 12 sts in the row).
Sew up the side of the mittens using invisible stitches, with blue or brown yarn and a tapestry needle.

Orange and fawn openwork scarf

The combination of an open stitch and fluffy yarn suits this very long scarf perfectly. There are different kinds of mohair available. Before buying your balls of wool, rub one of them on your skin to make sure it doesn't itch.

MATERIALS AND TOOLS

4.5 mm crochet hook
Yarn A: 80 g medium-weight orange mohair
Yarn B: 50 g medium-weight fawn mohair

TENSION

13 sts x 7 rows = 10 x 10 cm

SIZE

42 cm (width) x 4.15 m (length)

Construction

With yarn B, make 22ch foundation chain.

Row 1: 1tr, *5ch, miss 1ch, 1tr into next ch, rep from * to end of row.

Rows 2–34: *5ch, 1tr into next arch, rep from * to end of row. Turn the work around.

Rows 35–118: Rep as above with yarn A.

Rows 119–153: Rep as above with yarn B. Fasten off.

TO FINISH

Sew in the loose threads and gently steam the scarf.

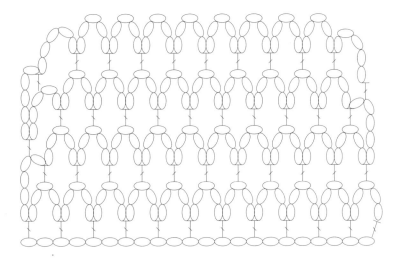

○ ch
⊤ tr

Net stitch diagram

Net swag

MATERIALS AND TOOLS

4.5 mm crochet hook

75 g orange mohair

95 cm leather drawstring, 2 mm wide

Fabric for swag lining: 120 x 25 cm

TENSION

13 sts x 7 rows = 10 x 10 cm

SIZE

26 cm wide at the base by
approx. 24 cm height

○ *ch*

T *tr*

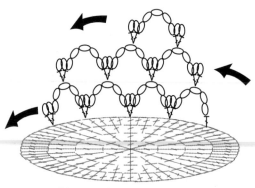

Diagram of the side of the bag

Construction

Make 6ch foundation chain, join with 1ss into the
1st ch to form a ring.
 2ch, 2tr into each ch.
Make 1ss into the 1st ch to close the round.
(12tr)
 2ch, *1tr, 2tr into the next tr, rep from * until you
have 18tr. Make 1ss in the 2nd ch to close the
round.
2ch, *1tr, 2tr into the next tr, rep from * until you
have 24tr. Make 1ss into the 2nd ch to close the
round.
Round 4, increase by 1ch every 4ch, Round 5,
increase by 1ch every 5ch, etc. until the 24th
round, when you should have 150tr, then begin the
side of the bag.

 1tr, *5ch, miss 3tr in last round of the base of the
bag, 1tr in next ch, 2ch, 1tr in same ch, rep from *
to end of round.
 *5ch, miss 2ch loop, 1tr in next loop, 2ch, 1tr in
same loop, rep from * to end of round.
 repeat 2nd round.
 *6ch, miss 2ch loop, 1tr in next arch, rep from *
to end of round.
 2ch, 1tr in each tr to end of round.

Cut the pieces for the lining as per the pattern.
Sew edges A and B together then sew the edge to
the base of the bag, distributing the fabric evenly
around the circle.
Slip the lining inside the mohair bag, wrong sides

continued >>>

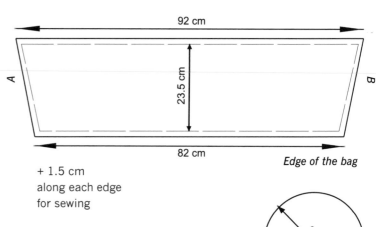

92 cm

23.5 cm

82 cm

A

B

Edge of the bag

+ 1.5 cm
along each edge
for sewing

25cm

Base

Patterns for the lining

facing, and join them together at the top of the
swag, by hand (blind stitch) or using a machine.
Thread the drawstring between the stitches of the
last row of the net stitch so that you can gather up
the top of the bag to close.

You can make a small swag for a child or a purse
based on the same design, or crochet a swag in
wool and felt it by washing at 40°C to give it a more
contemporary look.

Dog scarf

This silky scarf with pompoms on the end will charm any young girl. It has been made up in several colours, but it would also look lovely in black and would be especially elegant if you use only shades of brown.

MATERIALS AND TOOLS

10 mm knitting needles
10 mm crochet hook
Yarn A: 50 g fawn bouclé yarn
Yarn B: 55 g pink fluffy yarn
Yarn C: 55 g white fluffy yarn
2 black beads or 2 black buttons for the eyes
Orange wool or embroidery thread for the mouth and nose
Embroidery needle

TENSION

10 sts and 12 rows = 10 x 10 cm

SIZE

14 x 110 cm

Construction

SCARF

Cast on 12 sts.
Work *4 rows in garter stitch with yarn B, 4 rows in garter stitch with yarn C, rep 14 times from * (120 rows).
Cast off.

DOG'S HEAD

Using yarn A and the crochet hook, pick up 12 sts along the last row of the scarf.

Row 1: 2ch at the beginning of the row then 1tr in each of the next 11 sts.

Rows 2–8: Going back in the other direction, 2ch to turn, miss 1st tr then 1tr in each st to end of row.

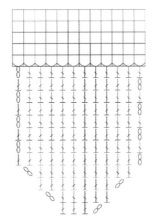

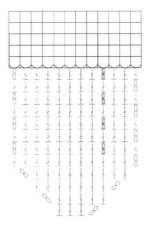

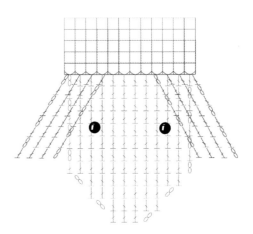

$\perp$ *tr*

0 *ch*

continued >>>

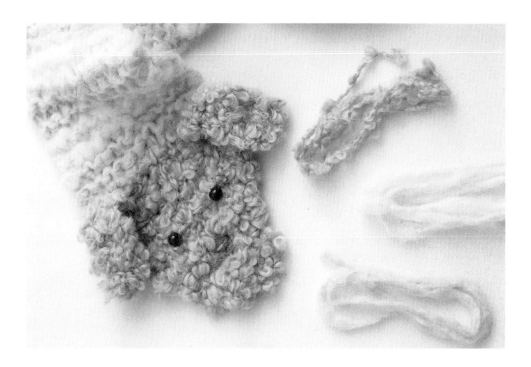

Rows 9–12: Decrease by 1tr at each end of the row as follows: 2ch to turn, miss 1st tr, yarn over hook, insert hook into next ch and draw 1 loop through, yarn over hook and draw through 1 loop (two loops on hook), yarn over hook, insert hook into next ch and draw 1 loop through, yarn over hook, draw it through 2 loops, yarn over hook, draw it through all loops on hook.

Continue in tr until there are 2tr and the turning ch left, decrease by 1tr and make the last tr by inserting hook into the turning ch.
Fasten off.

DOG EARS

With yarn A, pick up 4 sts on the 1st crocheted row of the dog head.

Row 1–8: 2ch to turn (counts as 1tr), miss 1st tr, 1tr in each ch to end of row. Fasten off.

TO FINISH

With yarn A, make a pompom (see opposite) 7 cm diameter and sew it on as the dog's tail.

Sew on the beads or buttons as eyes and embroider the nose and mouth with the orange thread. Gently steam the piece.

MAKING A POMPOM

Cut out two cardboard circles of the same diameter and cut out the middle to make two circlets. Place the two circlets on top of each other and wrap the wool around them until they are completely covered, and the centre hole is filled. Next, cut the wool around the external circumference by holding the centre in one hand and inserting the scissors between the two pieces of cardboard. Insert a piece of wool between the two pieces of cardboard and tie securely. Remove the pieces of cardboard and fluff up the wool to form the pompom.

Men's patchwork scarf

This design is particularly economical as it can be knitted using leftover yarn. It has been made using a double thickness of medium-weight yarn, but if you use very fine yarn, you can work with it tripled or quadrupled. Don't forget to make a tension square to check the effect it gives before knitting the scarf.

MATERIALS AND TOOLS

6.5 mm needles
Yarn A: 20 g mint green
Yarn B: 50 g brown
Yarn C: 50 g tomato red
Yarn D: 70 g khaki
Yarn E: 30 g grey
Yarn F: 80 g brick red
Yarn G: 60 g blue
Crochet hook or tapestry needle

TENSION

19 sts x 26 rows = 10 x 10 cm

SIZE

27 x 220 cm

Construction

The scarf is made up of four strips of two different widths in stocking and garter stitch, then sewn together. The colours are alternated as per the diagram. It is not essential for all the yarn to be the same thickness. Any differences will accentuate the patchwork effect of the piece.

continued >>>

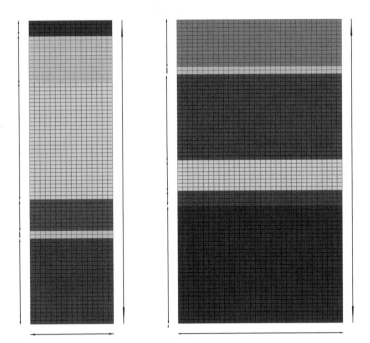

NARROW STRIP (MAKE 2)

With yarn B, cast on 16 sts and work 9 cm in stocking stitch.

With yarn A, work 1 cm in garter stitch.

With yarn F, work 3 cm in reverse stocking stitch.

With yarn D, work 12 cm in stocking stitch.

With yarn E, work 4 cm in reverse stocking stitch.

With yarn F, work 2 cm in reverse stocking stitch.

Repeat the design 3 times more (4 in all) for one strip, twice more (3 in all) for the other, then cast off.

WIDE STRIP (MAKE 2)

With yarn F, cast on 32 sts and work 12 cm in reverse stocking stitch.

With yarn B, work 1 cm in garter stitch.

With yarn D, work 3 cm in stocking stitch.

With yarn C, work 9 cm in reverse stocking stitch.

With yarn A, work 3 cm in reverse stocking stitch.

With yarn G, work 4 cm in stocking stitch.

Repeat the design 3 times more (4 in all) for one strip, twice more (3 in all) for the other, then cast off.

Place the strips side by side as per the diagram and join them together using yarn B, making a row of crochet or over-sewing them together with a tapestry needle. Sew in all of the loose threads and press gently with a steam iron.

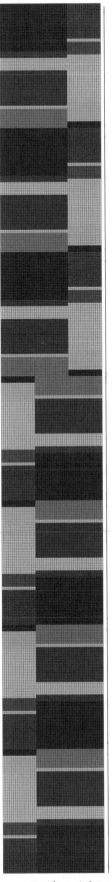

Autumn cap and scarf

This elegant cap is perfect for women with thick hair. Knit this ensemble in cashmere to take full advantage of its cosy softness.

MATERIALS AND TOOLS

3.5 mm, 4 mm and 4.5 mm needles
3 mm crochet hook
Medium-weight yarn containing cashmere
Scarf: 175 g
Cap: 125 g (using yarn doubled)
Leftover medium-weight yarn in violet, burgundy red and khaki for the berries, and bottle green for the leaves

TENSION

Hat: 21 sts and 30 rows = 10 x 10 cm
Scarf: 25 sts and 36 rows = 10 x 10 cm

SIZE

55 cm circumference x 33 cm

Construction

CAP

Using double yarn and 4 mm needles, cast on 104 sts.
Work 18 rows in single rib, increasing 4 sts evenly across the last row.
Change to 4.5 mm needles and work 50 rows in stocking stitch.

Decrease for crown as follows:

Row 1: *K10, K2tog, rep from * to end of row.
Row 2: Purl.
Row 3: *K9, K2tog, rep from * to end of row.
Row 4: Purl.
Continue decreasing in this manner every 2nd row until there are 9 stitches left.
Cut the yarn, thread it through the remaining stitches, draw up tightly and sew the edge of the hat with it.

SCARF

Using the 3.5 mm needles, cast on one stitch.
The border of the scarf is worked in garter stitch (all rows in knit).
Increase by 1 st either side of the cast-on stitch (3 sts).
In the next row, increase by 1 st either side of the middle stitch.
Increase by 1 st at each end of the next row, then every 2nd row until you have 32 sts.

continued >>>

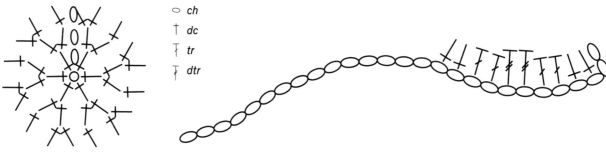

⌒	ch
†	dc
T	tr
T	dtr

Shape the central band as follows:

Next row: K15, inc by 1 st in each of the next 2 sts, K15.

Next row: K16, P2, K16.

Working the 16 sts in garter st on each edge, continue to increase 1 st at each side of the central stocking stitch panel in next and alternate rows, until you have 35 sts in the central panel. Continue straight for 654 rows, or until the total length of the scarf measures 170 cm.

Begin decreasing as follows:

Next row: K16, K2tog tbl (insert the needle through the back loops of the stitches), K31, K2tog, K16.

Continue to decrease 2 sts in every alternate row until 32 sts remain, then continue in garter st, decreasing as follows:

Next row: K1, K2tog, knit till 3 st from the end of the row, K2tog, K1. Continue to decrease at each end of every 2nd row until 1 st remains. Thread yarn through last st. Sew in loose threads and gently steam the piece to bring it into shape.

Make 7 berries for the scarf and 4 for the hat, following the instructions in the diagrams. Make 2 bottle-green leaves.

To assemble the berries, make a 15ch foundation chain, make 1ss into 1 berry, return along the length of the stem in dc to where you need to place the leaves. Sew the stems to the leaves and attach the whole piece to the scarf or hat using a few stitches or sew a safety pin to the back of the leaves to make a brooch.

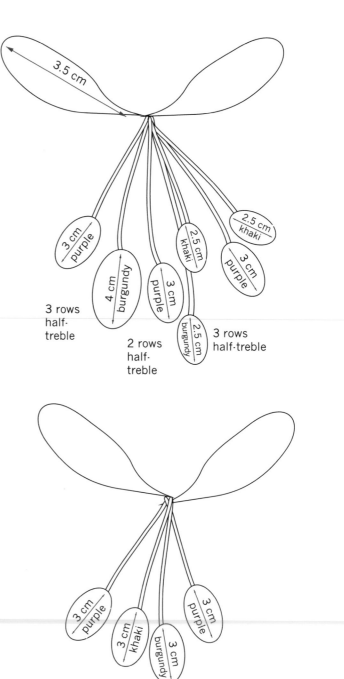

Stocking-stitch beanies for the whole family

These hats are very easy to knit and come together quickly. Make them in the size of your choice, plain or striped, and decorate them with pompoms, cherries or coloured circles, depending on who will be wearing them. Choose a soft and cuddly yarn to keep you nice and warm in winter.

MATERIALS AND TOOLS

Child's striped beanie:

4 mm and 4.5 mm needles

Hat: 20 g chocolate and 20 g pink medium-weight yarn

Pompoms: medium-weight yarn in chocolate, pink and brown, 10 g per pompom

Child's blue beanie:

3 mm crochet hook

40 g blue medium-weight yarn

Leftover medium-weight yarn for the crochet circles

Baby beanie:

3 mm crochet hook

25 g medium-weight red yarn

5 g medium weight green yarn

5 g red fancy yarn

TENSION

21 sts and 30 rows = 10 x 10 cm

SIZE

Child's beanies: 40 cm circumference x 20 cm height

Baby beanie: 32 cm circumference x 14.5 cm height

Striped beanie

Using 4 mm needles and the pink wool, cast on 104 sts. Work 12 rows in single rib, changing colour every 2nd row and increasing 2 sts evenly accross the last row. Change to 4.5 mm needles and work 26 rows in stocking stitch.

Decreasing for crown as follows:

Row 1: *K10, K2tog, rep from * to end of row.

Row 2: Purl.

Row 3: *K9, K2tog, rep from * to end of row.

Row 4: Purl.

Continue to decrease in this manner every 2nd row until there are 9 sts left.

Cut yarn, thread it through remaining sts, pull up tightly and use it to sew the edge of the beanie.

FINISHING

Make 2 chocolate pompoms, 4 cm diameter, 2 brown pompoms, 4 cm diameter and 3 pink pompoms, 2 cm diameter.

Sew the pompoms together. Cut several lengths of yarn, approximately 20 cm, fold them in two, attach them to the back of the pompoms and sew the whole arrangement close to the rim of the beanie.

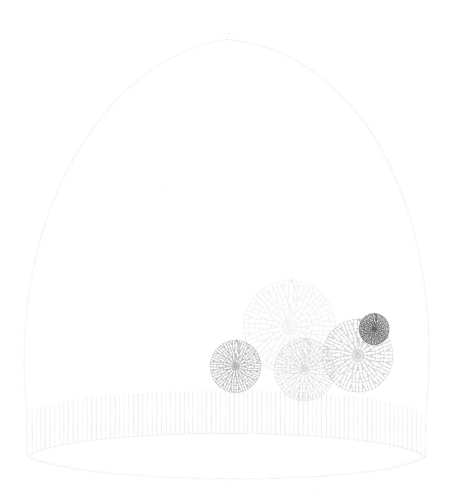

Blue beanie decorated with coloured circles

Cast on 82 sts using 4 mm needles.

Work 12 rows in single rib, increasing 2 sts evenly across last row.

Change to 4.5 mm needles and work 26 rows in stocking stitch.

Decrease and finish as for the previous beanie.

Crochet 5 circles in different colours and sizes and sew them onto the front of the beanie.

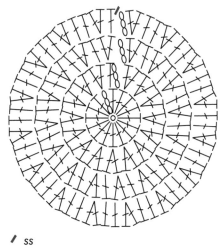

/ ss

○ ch

T tr

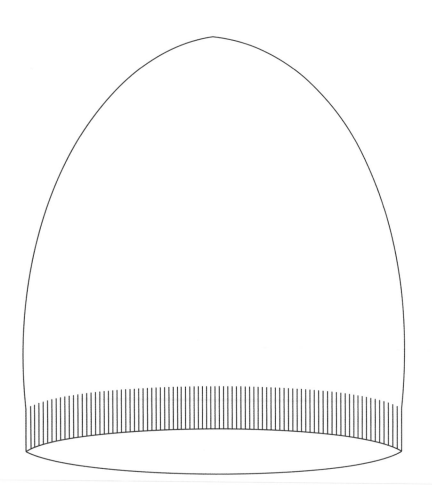

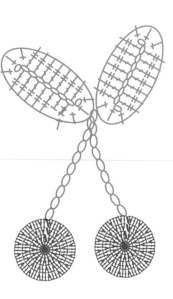

Baby beanie

Using 4 mm needles, cast on 66 sts.

Work 4 cm in single rib, increasing 6 sts evenly across the last row.

Change to 4.5 mm needles and work 14 rows in stocking stitch.

Decrease and finish the beanie as for the previous beanies.

To make the cherries, crochet 2 balls, 2 cm in diameter.

For the leaves, make a 9ch foundation chain and make 7 tr on each side, then make 1tr in dc all around the leaf. For the stem, make an 8 cm foundation chain, attach 1 cherry to each end then sew the leaves and the middle of the stem to the front of the beanie.

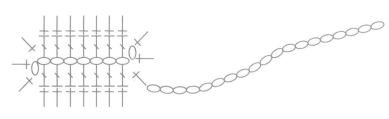

○ ch
⊥ dc
T tr

Men's scarf in garter stitch

This scarf is knitted using two yarns of different weights. If you don't find any suitable heathered yarn, combine several fine yarns together to make up a yarn that's the right colour and weight, then use it doubled.

MATERIALS AND TOOLS
4 mm needles
90 g brown medium-weight heathered yarn
40 g tweed yarn

TENSION
15 sts and 23 rows = 10 x 10 cm

SIZE
165 x 18 cm

Construction

This piece is knitted in garter stitch (all rows in knit).
Double up the tweed yarn and cast on 26 sts.
Work 5 rows in garter stitch.
Change yarn and work 5 rows in garter stitch using the brown heathered yarn.
Work 2 rows using the tweed yarn. Repeat, alternating the yarns and running the inactive yarn along the edge of the work.
Work a length of approx. 165 cm, finishing with 5 rows in tweed yarn.
Cast off all sts and sew in the loose threads.

Chapter 3

wraps

Basketweave stitch poncho and hairband

This poncho is just as suitable for a young girl as an adult. The child's version is decorated with a pretty crocheted picot edging, while the adult version has a plainer finish, but feel perfectly free to finish them in the same way.

TOOLS
6.5 mm needles
3 mm crochet hook

RED CHILD'S PONCHO AND HAIRBAND
Yarn A: 55 g red lambswool (used double)
Yarn B: 55 g red angora

GREY ADULT PONCHO
Yarn A: 125 g dark grey lambswool
(used double)
Yarn B: 100 g black angora

TENSION
16 sts and 30 rows = 10 x 10 cm

SIZE
Adult poncho: 100 cm (width) x 86 cm (height)
Child's poncho: 53 cm (width) x 49 cm (height)
Hairband: 85 cm long

continued >>>

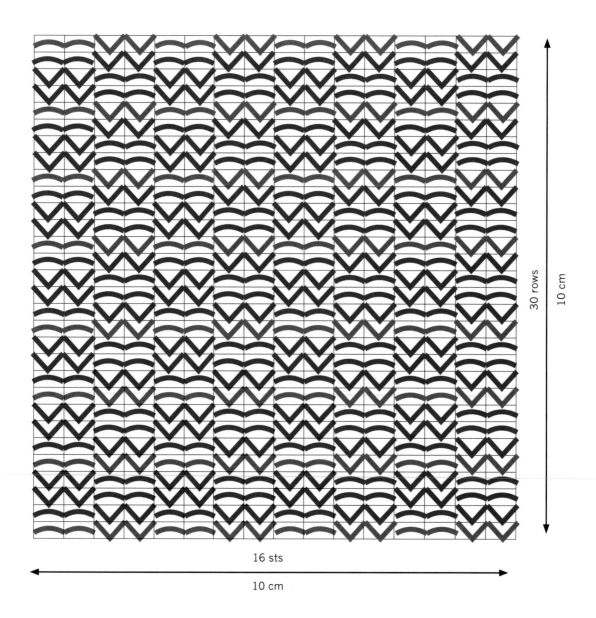

30 rows

10 cm

16 sts

10 cm

ᵛ   knit

⌒   purl

ᵛ⌒ yarn 1

⌒ᵛ yarn 2

Construction

PONCHO

The following instructions are given in two sizes. The 1st figure is for the child's size and the 2nd figure, given between parentheses, is for the adult size.

Cast on 46 (86) sts with yarn A, used double.

Rows 1 and 2: *K2, P2, rep from * to end of row.

Row 3: With yarn B, *P2, K2, rep from * to end of row.

Row 4: With yarn A, *P2, K2, rep from * to end of row.

Repeat these 4 rows, alternating 3 rows in yarn A (used double) and 1 row in yarn B, until you have 104 (200) rows in total. Cast off the stitches knitwise or purlwise as they appear. Make a 2nd identical panel and sew the two panels together, leaving an opening for the head.

For the adult poncho, using the 3 mm crochet hook and a length of yarn A, crochet 3 rows dc around the neck opening and at the bottom of the poncho.

For the child's poncho, crochet 2 rows dc with yarn A and crochet a picot edging by proceeding as follows:

Round 1: Work dc all around the poncho and use 1ss to close the round.

Round 2: 3dc, *4ch, 1ss in the base stitch of the picot, 3dc, rep from * to end of round. Proceed in the same way around the neck opening.

Sew in the loose threads and gently steam the garment.

continued >>>

HAIRBAND

Cast on 12 sts.

With yarn B, work in garter stitch (all rows in knit), increasing 1 st at each end of the first row (14 sts).

Work 19 more rows in garter stitch.

Next row: Inc 1 st at each end (16 sts).

Next 3 rows: Knit.

Continue in basketweave stitch as follows:

Row 1: Inc 1 st at each end (18 sts).

Rows 2–4: As per the diagram on page 76.

Row 5: Inc 1 st at each end (20 sts).

Rows 6–8: As per the diagram.

Row 9: Inc 1 st at each end (22 sts).

Rows 10–12: As per the diagram.

Row 13: Inc 1 st at each end (24 sts).

Rows 14–16: As per the diagram.

Row 17: Inc 1 st at each end (26 sts).

Row 18: As per the diagram.

Row 19: Inc 1 st at each end (28 sts).

Row 20: As per the diagram.

Row 21: Inc 1 st at each end (30 sts).

Row 22: As per the diagram.

Keeping pattern correct, work 24 rows without increase.

Row 47: As per the diagram.

Row 48: Dec 1 st at each end (28 sts).

Row 49: As per the diagram.

Row 50: Dec 1 st at each end (26 sts).

Row 51: As per the diagram.

Row 52: Dec 1 st at each end (24 sts).

Rows 53–55: As per the diagram.

Row 56: Dec 1 st at each end (22 sts).

Rows 57–59: As per the diagram.

Row 60: Dec 1 st at each end (20 sts).

Rows 61–63: As per the diagram.

Row 64: Dec 1 st at each end (18 sts).

Rows 65–67: As per the diagram.

Row 68: Dec 1 st at each end (16 sts).

Continue using yarn A and work 3 rows in garter stitch.

Next row: Dec 1 st at each end (14 sts).

Work 19 rows in garter stitch.

Next row: Dec 1 st at each end (12 sts).

Cast off.

PICOT EDGING

Using 3 mm crochet hook and yarn A, pick up 1 st at the edge of the garter stitch section and make 1ch.

Row 1: Work dc all around the hairband and use 1ss to close.

Row 2: 3dc, *4ch, 1ss into the base stitch of the picot, 3dc, rep from * to end of row.

Do the same thing on the other side of the hairband.

Sew in the loose ends and gently steam the piece.

Openwork crocheted shawl

This crochet stitch is called 'love knot' or 'Solomon's knot'. This quick-to-make shawl hangs perfectly due to its edging. Make it up in three colours, as here, or entirely in black, to cloak yourself in mystery.

MATERIALS AND TOOLS

4.5 mm crochet hook
Yarn A: 50 g pink mohair
Yarn B: 30 g brown mohair
Yarn C: 25 g burgundy mohair

SIZE

120 x 100 x 100 cm

SOLOMON'S KNOT

1 – Lengthen the loop on the hook until it measures 2.5 cm, yarn over hook, draw the yarn through the crochet loop.

2 – Insert hook under the left thread, behind the loop, yarn over hook, draw the thread through.

3 – Yarn over hook, draw the thread through the 2 crochet loops.

4 – Start the next stitch.

5 – Row 1, insert hook into 1ch out of 4 in the base chain. In the next rows, insert hook into the Solomon's knots of the preceding row.

6 – The last ch brings together the 4ch arranged in a diamond shape.

Construction

With yarn A, make a 150ch foundation chain and crochet 37 rows, decreasing by 1 st each side in every 2nd row. Fasten off.
With yarn B, crochet approx 150dc along the first side of the shawl and 130dc along the other 2 sides.
With yarn C, create a picot edging (see instructions for the edging of the child's poncho page 81). Fasten off the work and sew in loose ends.

continued >>>

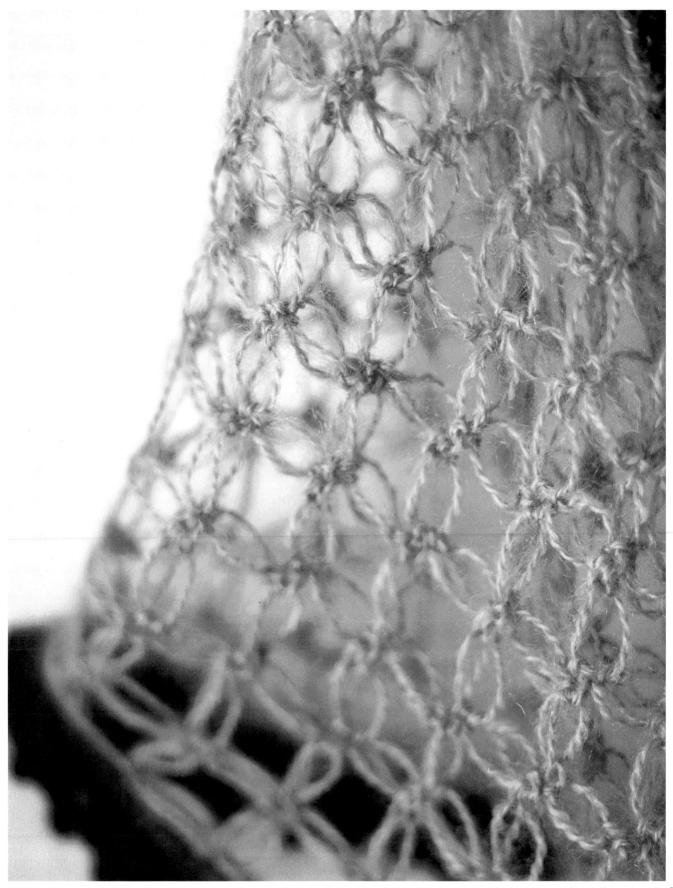

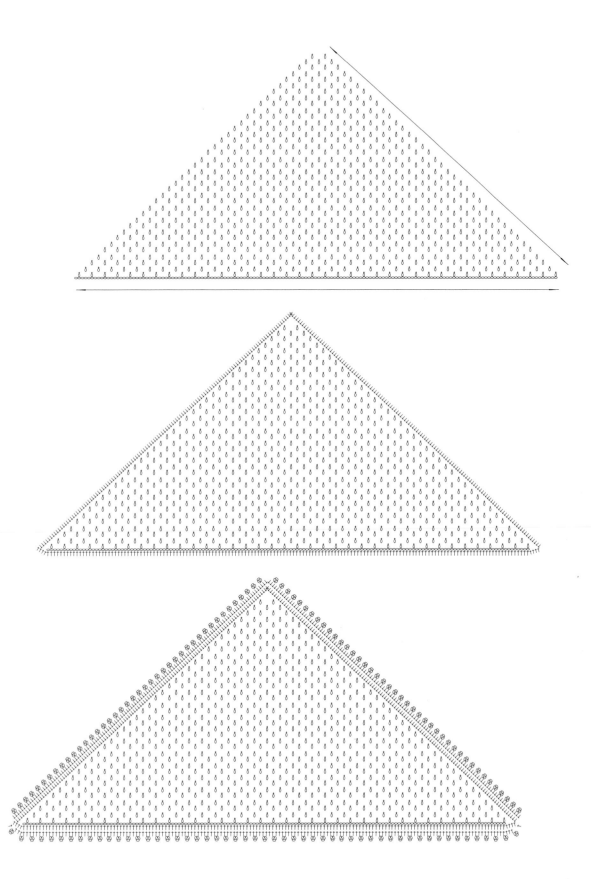

jumpers and cardigans

Tank top with appliqué

This little knitted top can be decorated with any kind of appliquéd motif. Reproduce one of the six motifs that follow in your choice of colours, or create your own decorative motif for even more originality.

MATERIALS AND TOOLS

4 mm and 5 mm needles
3.5 mm crochet hook
Yarn A: 100 g medium-weight yellow wool
Yarn B: 20 g medium-weight brown wool
Lightweight felt remnants
Embroidery thread
Embroidery needle
2 small buttons

TENSION

19 sts and 30 rows = 10 x 10 cm

SIZE

24 cm (height) x 26.5 cm (width)

Construction

BACK

With yarn B and the 4 mm needles, cast on 48 sts and work 2 rows in single rib.
With yarn A, work 8 rows in single rib.
Change to the 5 mm needles and work 36 rows in stocking stitch.

Armholes

Cast off 2 sts at each end of the next row, then 1 st at each end of every 2nd row, 4 times (36 sts).
Continue straight for 20 more rows.

Neck

K8, cast off the 20 middle sts, knit the 8 remaining stitches in the row.
Dec 1 st one stitch before the edge on the neck side in the next 2 rows. Cast off.
Join in yarn on the other side of the neck and repeat, reversing the decreases.

FRONT

Proceed as for the Back, to the end of the decreases for the armholes then work 10 rows straight.

Neck

K11, cast off the 14 middle stitches, knit to the end of the row.
Cast off 1 st on the neck side in the next row, then in every 3rd row until there are 7 sts remaining.
Work 5 more rows and cast off.
Join in yarn on the other side of the neck opening and repeat, reversing the neck decreases.
Work 8 more rows and cast off.

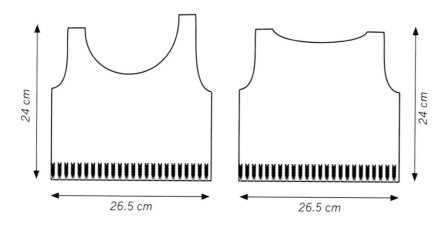

24 cm

26.5 cm

24 cm

26.5 cm

TO FINISH

Place the pieces on top of each other, right sides facing, and sew up the sides and the right shoulder.

With yarn B and the 3.5 mm crochet hook, make a picot edging around the right armhole, then around the left armhole and around the neck opening, making 2tr at the top of the front of the left shoulder so that you can button up the garment.

Picot edging

With yarn A and 3 mm hook, pick up 1 st and work 1ch around the edge of the garment.

Row 1: Work dc all around the armhole or neck hole and, for the right armhole, use 1ss in the 1st ch to close the round.

Row/Round 2: 3dc, *4ch, reinsert the hook into the base stitch of the picot, 3dc, rep from * to end of row.

Sew 2 buttons on the top of the back of the left shoulder. Sew in loose threads and gently steam the garment.

Copy the chosen motif onto paper or cardboard. Cut out the template and use it to cut out the shape in lightweight felt. Pin the felt motif to the top and sew around the edges using small stitches.

Decorate the motif in a contrasting thread, using the examples shown opposite as inspiration.

Little girl's smock

This little smock is quick to make because it is knitted with a thick yarn and large needles. Use smaller or larger needles according to the size of your model and use the ties to adjust the finished garment.

MATERIALS AND TOOLS

5 mm and 6 mm needles
3 mm crochet hook
Yarn A: 100 g chunky purple yarn
Yarn B: 100 g chunky chocolate yarn
Yarn C: 70 g chunky green yarn
Stitch holders

TENSION

14 sts and 18 rows = 10 x 10 cm

SIZE

47 cm (width) x 35 cm (height)
Size: around 3 years

Construction

BACK

With yarn B and the 6 mm needles, cast on 66 sts and work 4 rows in garter stitch (all rows in knit).
Join in yarn C and knit 1 row. Join in yarn A and purl 1 row. Take yarn B and knit 1 row. Continue in stocking stitch for 30 rows, repeating this alternation of colours.
Next row: Dec 1 st every 4 sts (50 sts). Change to 5 mm needles and continue in single rib for 6 rows, continuing to alternate the colours.

Armholes

Next row: Cast off 2 sts at each end.
Work 1 row in single rib.
Continue next row in single rib, decreasing 1 st each end (44 sts).
Work 19 rows in single rib and cast off.

FRONT

Proceed as for the Back to the end of the armhole decreases (44 sts).
Work 1 row in single rib.

Neckhole

Work 22 sts in single rib, transfer the remaining 22 sts onto a stitch holder, turn the work around.
Work 12 rows in single rib, continuing the stripes.

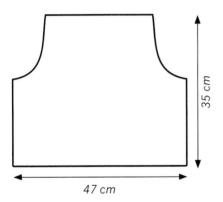

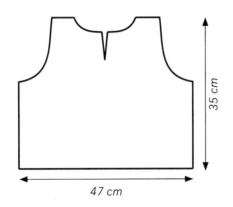

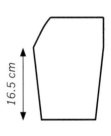

Next row: Cast off 5 sts on the neckhole side (17 sts).

Work 1 row in single rib.

Cast off 4 sts on the neckhole side of the next row, and following alternate.

Cast off the remaining 9 sts.

Pick up the stitches on the stitch holder and repeat as for the other side, reversing the decreases.

SLEEVES

With yarn B and the 6 mm needles, cast on 32 sts and work 4 rows in garter stitch (all rows in knit).

Change to 5 mm needles and continue in single rib, creating stripes as previously.

Increase 1 st at the beginning of the row every 4 rows, 7 times (39 sts).

Continue making the stripes for 30 rows, or until the sleeve measures 16.5 cm.

Cast off 3 sts at the beginning of the next row, and following 2 alternate rows.

Cast off the remaining 30 sts.

Make the second sleeve, reversing the increases and decreases by working them on the wrong side.

TO FINISH

Join the shoulders and sides. Sew up the seam along the under side of the sleeves, turn the body inside-out, wrong side outwards, and slip the sleeves into the armholes. Pin the sleeves to the armholes, then sew them into place using backstitch, without pulling the thread too tight. Make a double crochet edging around the neckhole. To make the ties, make an 80ch foundation chain then 1ss in each ch.

Make 2 small 16ch chains at the end of the tie, to create a small tassel on each end.

Attach the ties to the side seams, below the armholes.

Tweed jacket

This short jacket featuring a large shawl collar was knitted in heathered yarn to imitate tweed, combining a parquet stitch and a basketweave stitch.

MATERIALS AND TOOLS

5.5 mm and 6.5 mm needles

725 g medium-weight heathered yarn (knitted double)

1 large button

TENSION

16 sts and 26 rows knitted in basketweave stitch using 5.5 mm needles and double yarn = 10 x 10 cm

16 sts and 20 rows knitted in parquet stitch using 6.5 mm needles and double yarn = 10 x 10 cm

SIZE

52 cm, measured from the shoulders

Construction

BACK

Using 5.5 mm needles and double yarn, cast on 86 sts.

Proceed in basketweave stitch, as follows:

Row 1: *K2, P2, rep from * to end of row.

Row 2: *P2, K2, rep form * to end of row.

Row 3: *P2, K2, rep form * to end of row.

Row 4: *K2, P2, rep from * to end of row.

These last 4 rows form basketweave stitch.

Work 10 rows in basketweave stitch, increasing 4 sts evenly across the last row (90 sts).

Change to 6.5 mm needles and work 68 rows in parquet stitch, following the diagram, opposite.

ARMHOLES

Cast off 2 sts at the beginning of the next 2 rows.

Next row: K1, K2tog, work to last 3 sts, K2tog, K1.

Keeping parquet pattern correct, decrease 2 sts in every row until 68 sts remain.

Continue without shaping until work measures 18 cm from beginning of armhole.

Next row: Keeping pattern correct, work 2 sts, increase once in next st, work to last 3 sts, increase once in next st, work 2 sts.

Repeat last row twice more (74 sts).

Continue without shaping until work measures 22 cm from beginning of armhole.

continued >>>

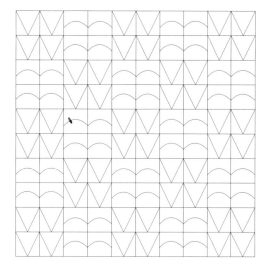

Basketweave stitch

∨ *knit*

   purl

Parquet stitch

Next row: Work 27 sts, cast off next 20 sts for neck opening, turn.

Next row: Decrease 1 st at neck edge in this and following alternate rows until 24 sts remain.

Cast off.

Join in yarn to remaining sts and complete to correspond with other side, reversing shaping.

FRONT

Using 5.5 mm needles and double yarn, cast on 50 sts.

Work 10 rows in basketweave stitch, as for Back.

Change to 6.5 mm needles and continue in parquet stitch for 68 rows.

Following the instructions for the Back, shape an armhole in one edge and continue until work measures 15 cm from beginning of armhole.

To make the neck opening on the other edge, decrease 1 st at the beg of every 2nd row, at the same time keeping the armhole shaping correct, until there are 24 sts remaining.

Cast off.

Work second Front to correspond with first, reversing shaping.

SLEEVES

Using 5.5 mm needles and double yarn, cast on 60 sts.

Work 10 rows in basketweave stitch, as for Back.

Change to 6.5 mm needles and parquet stitch, increasing 1 st at each end of every 6th row until you have 86 sts.

Continue without shaping until Sleeve measures 50 cm (or the desired measurement from wrist to armhole.)

Cast off 2 sts at the beginning of the next 2 rows.

Decrease 1 st at the beginning and end of the next and every alternate row until 70 sts remain, then in every row until 16 sts remain. Cast off.

Work a second Sleeve to match the first.

Sew the sleeves to the armholes, then sew the sleeve and side seams.

FRONT BAND AND COLLAR

Using 5.5 mm needles and double yarn, cast on 20 sts. Work in basketweave stitch until work measures about 40 cm (or to the bottom of the neck opening).

Increase 1 st in the last st of the next and every alternate row, until the Band reaches the centre back of the neck edge and the collar measures 25 cm across.

Make a second Band in the same way.

Sew the two Bands together at the centre back neck edge, using a flat seam, then attach the Collar to the jacket. Crochet a button loop and attach loop and button to Collar.

Chapter 5

tootsies

Woollen slippers are perfect for keeping feet toasty warm when you're staying in. The following designs are varied enough for everyone to find one they like.

The slippers on this page have been felted. Knit them up in pure wool and wash them at 60°C to obtain the same result.

Red slippers in garter stitch

MATERIALS AND TOOLS

5.5 mm needles

60 g medium-weight red wool

SIZE

Before felting: 20 x 10 cm

(after felting: 12.5 x 8 cm)

TENSION

25 sts and 23 rows = 10 x 10 cm

Construction

Cast on 59 sts.

Row 1 and all odd rows: Knit.

Row 2: K29 to the middle st, inc 2 sts, knit to end of row.

Row 4: K30, inc 1 st, K1, inc 1 st, knit to end of row.

Row 6: K30, inc 1 st, K3, inc 1 st, knit to end of row.

Row 8: K30, inc 1 st, K5, inc 1 st, knit to end of row.

Row 10: K30, inc 1 st, K7, inc 1 st, knit to end of row.

Row 12: K30, inc 1 st, K9, inc 1 st, knit to end of row.

Row 14: K30, inc 1 st, K11, inc 1 st, knit to end of row.

Row 16: K30, inc 1 st, K13, inc 1 st, knit to end of row.

Work 27 rows garter st without increasing.

Cast off 12 sts at the beginning of next 2 rows.

Work a further 12 rows in garter st without shaping.

Decreasing row: K1, sl 1, psso, knit to last 3 sts, K2tog, K1.

Work 9 rows in garter st without shaping.

Next decreasing row: K1, sl 1, psso, K10, sl 1, psso, K11, K2tog, K10, K2tog, K1.

Work 7 rows in garter st without shaping.

Next decreasing row: K1, sl 1, psso, K8, sl 1, psso, K9, K2tog, K8, K2tog, K1.

Work 3 rows in garter st without shaping.

Next decreasing row: K1, sl 1, psso, knit to last 3 sts, K2tog, K1.

Work 1 row in garter st without shaping.

Next decreasing row: K1, sl 1, psso, K6, sl 1, psso, K5, K2tog, K10, K2tog, K1.

Work 5 rows in garter st without shaping.

Cast off.

Make a second slipper to match the first. Sew the slippers up by grafting the seams (see page 106), making sure to keep the seams quite flat.

Technique: grafting

Grafting is a technique that enables two pieces of knitting to be joined together with a seam that looks like a row of stitches, and has the advantage of making the seams invisible. It is used on pieces that end with a selvedge or with stitches left waiting on a stitch holder.

Place the pieces to be joined together on a flat surface, one beside the other, and, using a tapestry needle and the same yarn as used for the work, pick up a stitch of one piece then the corresponding stitch on the piece opposite. Continue in this way all along the seam, pulling the thread so that it forms stitches that are identical to those in the work.

When making this seam, make sure you use a piece of yarn that's long enough for the whole seam (about three times the length of the seam being made).

Slippers with button strap

This charming pattern can also be made without the button strap.

MATERIALS AND TOOLS
5.5 mm needles
35 g medium-weight yarn
2 buttons (optional)

SIZE
13 x 6.5 cm

Construction

Cast on 23 sts.
Row 1 and every odd row: Knit.
Row 2: K11 to the middle st, inc 2 sts, knit to end of row.
Row 4: K11, inc 1 st, K3, inc 1 st, knit to end of row.
Row 6: K11, inc 1 st, K5, inc 1 st, knit to end of row.
Row 8: K11, inc 1 st, K7, inc by 1 st, knit to end of row.
Row 10: K11, inc 1 st, K9, inc 1 st, knit to end of row.
Row 12: K11, inc 1 st, K11, inc 1 st, knit to end of row (35 sts).
Knit 19 rows without shaping.
Decreasing row: K1, sl1, psso, knit to last 3 sts, K2tog, K1.
Knit 15 rows without shaping.
Decreasing row: K1, sl1, psso, knit to last 3 sts, K2tog, K1.
Knit 3 rows without shaping.

Next decreasing row: K1, sl1, psso, K11, K2tog, K5, K2tog, K1.
Knit 3 rows without shaping.
Next decreasing row: K1, sl1, psso, K4, sl1, psso, K9, K2tog, K4, K2tog, K1.
Knit 3 rows without shaping.
Next decreasing row: K1, sl1, psso, knit to last 3 sts, K2tog, K1.
Knit 1 row and cast off.
Make a 2nd identical slipper. Make the slippers up by grafting (see page 106), making sure the seams are quite flat.

BUTTON STRAPS
Cast on 18 sts and work 6 rows in garter stitch. Cast off.
Sew the button straps to the top of the slippers, leaving an opening for the button.

Slipper-socks

MATERIALS AND TOOLS

5.5 mm needles

Medium-weight yarn, 100 g for Size 1 (50 g for size 2)

TENSION

26 sts and 24 rows = 10 x 10 cm

SIZE

Size 1: 17 x 19 cm (size 2: 13 x 13 cm)

The instructions for Size 1 are given first, followed by those for Size 2 (smaller) given between parentheses.

Construction

Cast on 81 (67) sts.

Row 1 and every odd row: Knit.

Row 2: K40 (34) to the middle st, inc by 2 sts, knit to end of row.

SIZE 1 ONLY

Row 4: K40, inc 1 st, K1, inc 1 st, knit to end of row.

Row 6: K40, inc 1 st, K3, inc 1 st, knit to end of row.

Row 8: K40, inc 1 st, K5, inc 1 st, knit to end of row.

Row 10: K40, inc 1 st, K7, inc 1 st, knit to end of row.

Row 12: K40, inc 1 st, K9, inc 1 st, knit to end of row.

Row 14: K40, inc 1 st, K11, inc 1 st, knit to end of row.

Row 16: K40, inc 1 st, K13, inc 1 st, knit to end of row (97 sts).

SIZE 2 ONLY

Row 4: K11, inc 1 st, K3, inc 1 st, knit to end of row.

Row 6: K11, inc 1 st, K5, inc 1 st, knit to end of row.

Row 8: K11, inc 1 st, K7, inc 1 st, knit to end of row.

Row 10: K11, inc 1 st, K9, inc 1 st, knit to end of row.

Row 12: K11, inc 1 st, K11, inc 1 st, knit to end of row.

SIZE 1 AND 2

Knit 23 (19) rows without shaping.

Decreasing row: K28 (22) sl1, psso, K36 (29), K2tog, knit to end of row.

Knit 3 rows without shaping.

Cast off 27 (21) sts at each end of the next row.

Knit 11 (11) rows without shaping.

Decreasing row: K1, sl1, psso, to last 3 sts, K2tog, K1.

Knit 9 (3) rows without shaping.

Next decreasing row: K1, sl1, psso, K10 (5), sl1, psso, K11 (10), K2tog, K10 (5), K2tog, K1.

Knit 7 (3) rows without shaping.

Next decreasing row: K1, sl1, psso, K8 (4), sl1, psso, K9, K2tog, K8 (4), K2tog, K1.

Knit 3 rows without shaping.

Next decreasing row: K1, sl1, psso, knit to last 3 sts, K2tog, K1.

Knit 1 row (Cast off all the stitches for Size 2).

Next decreasing row: K1, sl1, psso, K6, sl1, psso, K5, K2tog, K10, K2tog, K1.

Knit 5 rows and cast off.

Make a 2nd identical slipper. Make up the slippers by grafting (see page 106), making sure to keep the seams nice and flat.

Chapter 6

bags

Angora patchwork bag

This multicolour bag is perfect for using up leftover fabric and yarn. Its originality is further enhanced by golden seam.

MATERIALS AND TOOLS

3 mm crochet hook

Yarn A: 20 g medium-weight dark grey lambswool (for 5 squares)

Yarn B: 20 g moss green angora wool (for 5 squares)

Yarn C: 30 g medium-weight chocolate lambswool (for 4 squares and the handles)

Yarn D: 15 g maroon angora wool (for 4 squares)

Yarn E: 20 g dark green medium-weight lambswool (for 4 squares)

Yarn F: 20 g medium-weight metallic gold yarn

Enough flannel to make a lining for 22 squares with 8 cm sides

TENSION

Lambswool squares:

16 dc and 15 rows = 8 x 8 cm

Angora squares:

15 dc and 16 rows = 8 x 8 cm

SIZE

Approximately 28 cm (width) x 25 cm (length, not including handles)

Lambswool squares

Make a 16ch foundation chain.

Row 1: 1ch to turn, miss 1st ch from the hook, 1dc into each ch to end of row (16sts).

Rows 2–15: 1ch, miss 1st dc, 1dc into each ch to end of row (16dc).

Angora squares

Make a 15ch foundation chain.

Row 1: 1ch to turn, miss 1ch from the hook, 1dc into each ch to end of row (15 sts).

Row 2–16: 1ch, miss the 1st dc, 1 dc into each st to end of row (15 sts).

Angora *Lambswool*

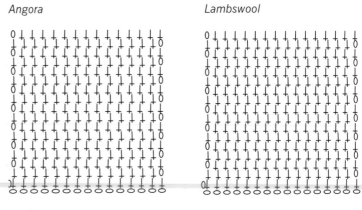

o ch

↓ dc

continued >>>

TO ASSEMBLE THE SQUARES

Arrange the squares as per the diagram on the next page, and crochet together using double crochet with the gold yarn.

HANDLES

With yarn C, make a 105ch foundation chain.

Rows 1–3: 1ch to turn, miss the 1st st, 1 dc into each ch to end of row (105 sts).

Rows 4 and 5: With yarn F, 1ch to turn, miss the 1st st from the hook, 1 dc in each st to end of row (105 sts).

Rows 6–8: With yarn C, 1ch, miss the 1st st, 1 dc into each st to end of row (105 sts).

TO MAKE THE LINING

Cut out the lining using the assembly pattern opposite as a template (1 square = 8 cm per side).

Slip the fabric bag inside the crochet bag, wrong sides facing, and sew them together at the top of the bag, taking the handles into the seam (the latter will be invisible from the outside of the bag).

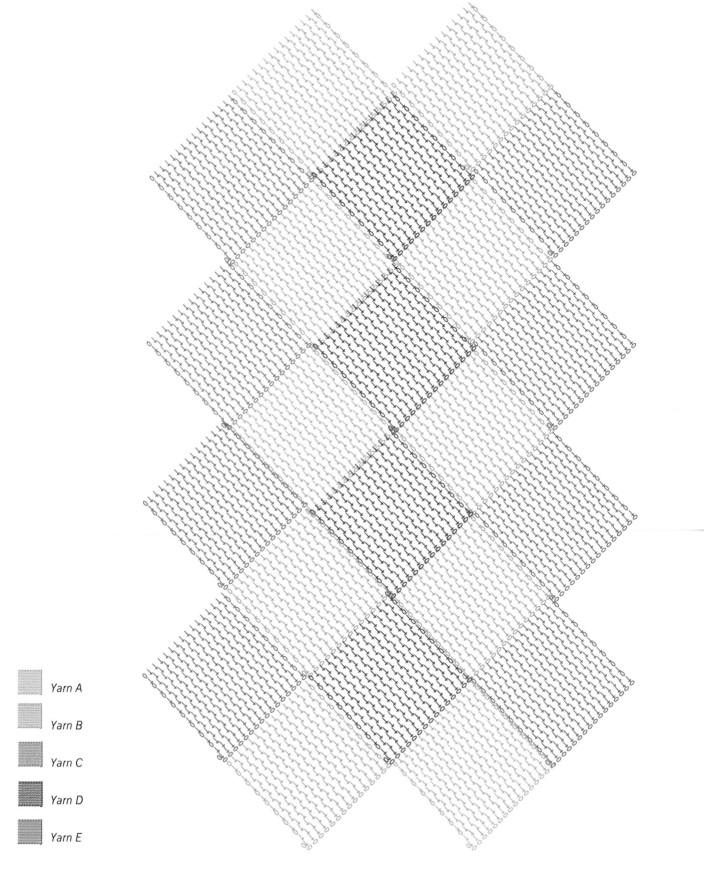

Yarn A

Yarn B

Yarn C

Yarn D

Yarn E

Ringed pockets

These pockets are perfect for protecting a powder compact from getting scratches or, worse, opening up inside a handbag. They are made by covering curtain rings, like those you may have kept in the bottom of a drawer or sewing bag.

MATERIALS AND TOOLS
3 mm crochet hook
Large Press stud
Embroidery needle

Pocket A:
32 rings, 25 mm diameter
1 ring, 12 mm diameter
10 g medium-weight wool yarn
18 x 31 cm green lightweight felt
20 x 35 cm printed cotton for the lining

Pocket B:
50 rings, 12 mm diameter
10 g yarn in various colours
14.5 x 22 cm yellow lightweight felt
16 x 25 cm printed cotton for the lining

SIZE
Pocket A: 18 x 15.5 cm
Pocket B: 14.5 x 11 cm

Pocket A

Make 2 rows of 8 rings with the red wool, following the diagram on the next page. To do this, make 16 dc around half of one 25 mm ring, repeat on the next ring, cover the 8th ring with 32dc then return along the row, covering the other half of the preceding rings.
Sew the 4 rows onto half of the felt and to each other.
Cover 1 small 12 mm ring using 20dc and attach it to the middle of the top of the pocket. Fold the lining fabric in half, right sides together, and sew up the edges by machine or hand, using back stitch. Fold a hem along the opening.

continued >>>

Fold the felt and attach it to the lining using blanket stitch along the seams and at the top of the piece. If needed, attach a press stud to the middle of the opening.

Pocket B

Make 5 rows of 10 rings following the diagram at right. Begin by making 10dc around each ring, changing colour for each ring. Cover the 10th ring with 20dc and go back along the band. Attach the rings to half of the felt and finish as per pocket A.

 dc

12 mm ring

25 mm ring

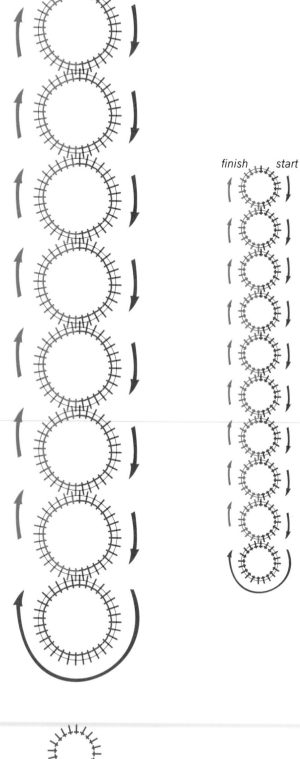

Zigzag purse

These little coloured purses are entirely crocheted in double and treble stitch. When changing colours, the new yarn is crocheted on top of the previous one and covers a number of treble stitches to create a certain thickness and make chevron shapes.

MATERIALS AND TOOLS

Medium-weight yarns in 6 different colours,
5 g each colour
1 button, 2.5 cm diameter

TENSION

22 sts and 37 rows = 10 x 10 cm

SIZE

10.5 cm x 8 cm

Zigzag stitch in crochet

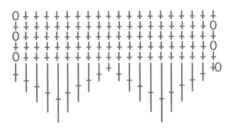

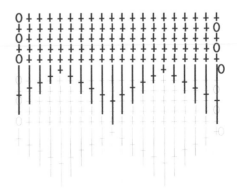

○ ch
+ dc
┼ tr

continued >>>

Construction

With yarn A, make a 22ch foundation chain.

Row 1: Make 1dc into the 3rd ch from the hook, 1dc in each ch to end of row. Turn.

Row 2: 1ch to turn (counts as the 1st dc), miss the 1st st, 1dc in each st. Turn.

Rows 3–6: Rep the 2nd row.

Row 7: Take yarn 2 and make 1ch. *1dc into the next st, missing 1 row, 1dc into the next st, missing 2 rows, 1dc into the next st, missing 3 rows, 1dc in the next st, missing 4 rows, 1dc into the next st, missing 5 rows, 1dc into the next st, missing 4 rows, 1dc missing 3 rows, 1dc missing 2 rows, 1dc missing 1 row, 1dc into the next st, rep from * to end of row.

Rows 8–12: With yarn 2, rep the 2nd row.

Row 13: Take yarn 3 and make 1ch, 1dc into the 1st st, missing 5 rows *1dc into the next st, missing 4 rows, 1dc into the next st, missing 3 rows, 1dc into the next st, missing 2 rows, 1dc into the next stitch, missing 1 row, 1tr into the next st missing 2 rows, 1tr into the next st, missing 3 rows, 1tr into the next st, missing 4 rows, 1tr into the next st, missing 5 rows, rep from * to end of row. Turn.

Rows 14–18: With yarn 3, rep the 2nd row.

Rep this zigzag motif, alternating the 6 colours until the piece measures approximately 20.5 cm (approx 75 rows) and fasten off. Fold up the rectangle as shown below.

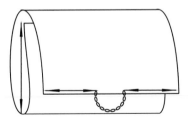

Crochet a dc edging, joining the edges together at the same time.

Attach a button to the front of the purse and crochet a treble stitch in the middle of the front flap: Pick up 1 st along the edge, make 10ch, miss 5 st and use 1ss to close the treble stitch.

When changing colour, you need to make sure you wind the working yarn around the others to make a neat edge.

Felted crocheted bag

This little handbag is very quick to make and is the perfect size for doing the shopping. It only needs a felted brooch to dress it up.

MATERIALS AND TOOLS

9 mm crochet hook
360 g pure wool (used double and quadruple)
Tapestry needle

TENSION

9 sts and 7 rows = 10 x 10 cm (after felting)
As not all yarns shrink at the same rate, you should start by making tension samples and washing them to check the effect before going ahead with the piece.

SIZE

24 x 39 cm (base: 11.5 x 36 cm)

Construction

BASE

Start by making the base of the bag: make a 10ch foundation chain and 27 rows dc using a quadruple thickness of wool.
Pick up 86 sts all around the base and crochet 20 rows dc.
In the last row, make 1 picot every 6 sts by proceeding as follows: *6dc, 4ch, reinsert the hook into the base stitch of the picot, rep from * all around the edge. Fasten off.

SIDES

Take a double thickness of yarn, make a 10ch foundation chain and make 16 rows dc. Crochet a second identical square. Sew the sides of the two squares together, then join to the base of the bag, using a tapestry needle and matching thread.

HANDLES

Using a double thickness of yarn, make a 5ch foundation chain and 20 rows in dc. Crochet a second handle identical to the first and sew the handles to the top of the bag. Sew in all of the loose ends then wash the bag at 60°C to felt, based on the rate at which your tension samples felted.

Chapter 7

home

Fluffy cloud cushions

These light and soft cushions will bring a touch of the sky to your interior. The largest requires lots of pompoms. Ask your children to help you or organise a 'pompom workshop' with friends while your feet are still on the ground…

MATERIALS AND TOOLS

Large cushion: For 120 pompoms, 3 cm diameter, 200 g very pale wool, for example white, cream, pale grey or pale pink
Fabric for the underside: 35 cm x 55 cm cream wool flannel
Fabric for the top: 35 cm x 55 cm cream satin

Medium cushion: For 30 pompoms, 5 cm in diameter, 150 g very pale wool, for example white, cream, pale grey or pale pink
Fabric for the underside: 30 cm x 50 cm fluffy cream fabric
Fabric for the top: 30 cm x 50 cm cream satin.

Small cushion: 10 g cream bulky slub yarn and 10 g fine cream wool
Fabric for the underside: 25 cm x 35 cm cream wool flannel
Fabric for the top: 25 cm x 35 cm cream satin

For all sizes: Polyester filling

Template for the pompoms
Tapestry needle

SIZE
Small cushion: 28 x 16 cm
Medium cushion: 42 x 25 cm
Large cushion: 50 x 29 cm

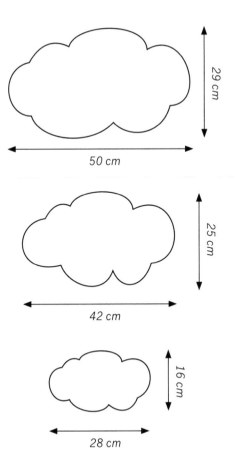

50 cm

29 cm

42 cm

25 cm

28 cm

16 cm

continued >>>

Construction

LARGE CUSHION

Cut out the top and bottom pieces of the
cushion using the large cloud-shaped template.
Sew both pieces together, right sides together,
leaving a 20-cm opening so that it can be
stuffed. Turn right side out.
Make 120 pompoms, 3 cm in diameter, and
sew them to the top of the cushion.
Stuff the cushion with filling and close the opening.

MEDIUM CUSHION

Cut out the top and bottom pieces of the cushion
using the medium-sized cloud-shaped template.
Sew both pieces together, right sides together,
leaving a 20-cm opening so that it can be
stuffed. Turn right side out.
Make 30 pompoms, 5 cm diameter, and sew
them to the top of the cushion.
Stuff the cushion with polyester filling and close
the opening.

SMALL CUSHION

Cut out the top and bottom pieces of the cushion
using the small cloud-shaped template. Using
the fine cream yarn, sew the chunky slub yarn to
the top of the cushion. Sew the top and bottom
together, right sides together, leaving a 20-cm
opening. Stuff with filling and close the opening.

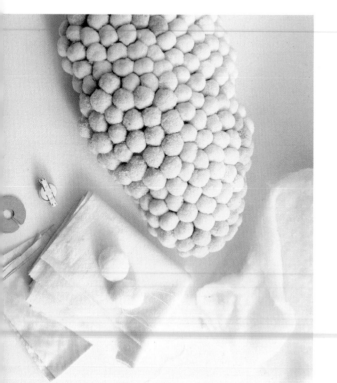

Crocheted carpet

Crocheted items are rarely designed to go on the floor but this warm and soft carpet will easily find a place inside your home. If you make it from pure wool and felt it when it is first washed, it will be even more beautiful and durable.

MATERIALS AND TOOLS

9 mm and 7 mm crochet hooks
Yarn 1 (main colour): 500 g chunky grey wool
Yarn 2: 20 g pale pink wool
Yarn 3: 20 g pale yellow wool
Yarn 4: 20 g green wool
Yarn 5: 20 g yellow-green wool
Yarn 6: 20 g turquoise wool
Yarn 7: 20 g bright pink wool

Construction

Large two-colour circle (make 16 times)

Using the 9 mm crochet hook and your choice of yarns 2 to 7, make a 16ch foundation chain, join with 1ss to form a ring.

Round 1: *4ch, 1tr into the base ring, rep from * until you have 16tr, close with 1ss.

Round 2: *1tr into 1tr, 4ch, miss 1tr, rep 7 times from * and close with 1ss (8 tr).

For the next 3 rounds, use yarn 1, begin each round with 3ch and join up the ring with 1ss.

Round 3: *3tr group, 3ch, rep 7 times from *.

Round 4: *3tr group, 1ch, 3tr group in the same arch, 3ch, rep 7 times from *.

Round 5: *3tr group in the next arch, 3ch, rep 15 times from *.

Round 6: Complete the whole round in dc, making 3dc into each 3ch arch and 1dc into each 3tr group.

Fasten off and sew in the loose threads.

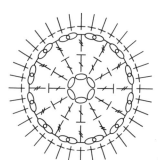

ch
dc
tr
dtr

continued >>>

 pale pink

yellow

 green

yellow-green

 bright pink

Small circle (make 9 times)

Using the 7 mm hook and yarn 1, make a 6ch foundation chain and join with 1ss to form a ring.

Round 1: 12tr into the base ring, close the round with 1ss.

Round 2: *1dtr into the next tr, 2ch, rep from * to end of round.

Round 3: 1dc into each st and fasten off.

Join up each small circle to 4 large circles, by hand, following the diagram.

Granny square bedspread

This large bed-cover is easy to make because it is made up of small individually-made squares. A ball of wool and crochet hook is all you need to work on the piece, wherever you are. The model opposite has been made using five natural shades but you can choose other colours to match it with your decor.

MATERIALS AND TOOLS

1 crochet hook
Yarn 1: 280 g ecru
Yarn 2: 280 g beige
Yarn 3: 280 g maroon
Yarn 4: 280 g grey
Yarn 5: 280 g oatmeal

TENSION

1 square: 8.5 x 8.5 cm

SIZE

200 x 175 cm

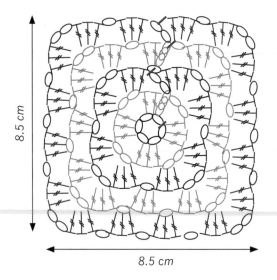

Making a square

Make a 6ch foundation chain and join with 1ss to form a ring.

Round 1: 3ch (counts as 1dtr), 2dtr into the ring, 2ch *3dtr, 2ch, rep 3 times from *.

Round 2: 2ch, (3dtr, 2ch, 3dtr) into the 1st chain loop for the corner. *1ch (3dtr, 2ch, 3dtr) into the next 2 chain loops, rep 2 more times from * and close the round with 1ss into the 2nd st from the beginning of the round.

Round 3: 3ch, 2dtr into the 1st chain loop, 1ch *(3dtr, 2ch, 3dtr) into the next 2ch loop, 1ch, 3dtr into the next 1ch loop, 1ch, rep 2 times from *, 3dtr, 2ch, 3dtr into the last 2ch loop, 1ch. Close the round with 1ss into the 3rd st from the beginning of the round.

Round 4: 2ch, 3dtr into the next 1ch loop, 1ch, *(3dtr, 2ch, 3dtr) into the next 2ch loop, 1ch, 2 times (3dtr into the next 1ch loop, 1ch), rep 2 times from *, (3dtr, 2ch, 3dtr) into the last 2ch loop, 1ch, 3dtr into the last 1ch loop. Close the round with 1ss into the 2nd st from the beginning of the round. Fasten off.

Crochet 44 squares in one colour and 45 in each of the others so that you have a total of 224 squares.

continued >>>

16 squares

14 squares

rep

rep

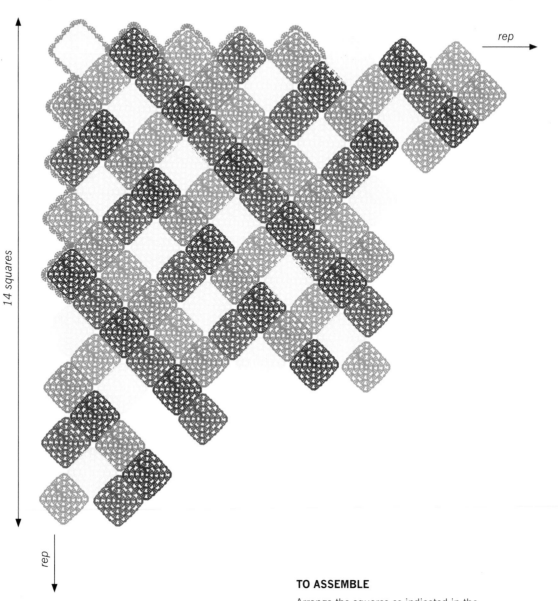

TO ASSEMBLE

Arrange the squares as indicated in the diagram.

With yarn 5 (or whichever you have the most leftover of), assemble the squares using slip stitch with a tapestry needle or using double crochet, with a crochet hook.

Make a scalloped edge all around the piece: pick up 1 st all around the edge, make 1ss, *miss 2ch, 6dtr into the same ch, 1ss into the next ch, rep from * all around the work.

Écru

 Beige

 Maroon

 Grey

 Oatmeal

137

Patchwork cushion

This little cushion is ideal for using the leftover materials you keep
with no particular project in mind.

MATERIALS AND TOOLS

Leftover pieces of ribbon
Tapestry wool and silk embroidery thread
Fabric remnants
Pieces cut out of old clothes
2 squares of fabric 30 x 30 cm for the lining
Buttons or rings
Cushion or polyester filling

SIZE

27 x 27 cm

Construction

Lay the squares for the lining out flat and arrange
on top the fabric remnants you have gathered
together, keeping in mind the balance of textures
and colours. Cut out the pieces as appropriate so
that they overlap slightly.
Once you are happy with the effect, pin and
baste each piece to the lining.
Use the wool and embroidery thread to decorate
the seams using decorative embroidery stitches
(herringbone stitch, blanket stitch, running
stitch, a row of French knots, etc.).
Add buttons or crocheted motifs using
leftover wool.

Place the top and underside of the cushion
together, right sides together, and sew up three
of the sides, leaving a 1.5 cm border. Turn the
piece right side out, slip a cushion inside or stuff
it and sew up the opening by hand.

Fancy cushions

Stretch out on your couch and admire these multicoloured cushions. Start by making coloured circles then arrange them on your cushion covers, taking inspiration from the examples shown opposite or following your own fancy...

MATERIALS AND TOOLS

Purple lightweight felt: 40 x 50 cm
Green lightweight felt: 40 x 10 cm
Tweed: 35 x 50 cm
Medium-weight purple yarn
Shiny fine purple yarn
Matte fine purple yarn
6 metal rings, approximately 1.5 cm or 5.2 cm in diameter
2 buttons for each cushion
Cushions to fill the covers
Tapestry needle
3 mm crochet hook
Awl or hole-punch

SIZE

Rectangular cushion: 30 x 40 cm
Square cushion: 30 x 30 cm

MAKING A CUSHION

Mark the size of the top cover of the cushion on the fabric and cut it out leaving a 1.5 cm border.
Cut out the desired number of circles in the felt according to the pattern. Pierce the edges of the circles with an awl or a hole-punch and, using the crochet hook, make a row of double crochet around each circle.
Crochet other circles, as desired, using the diagrams below.

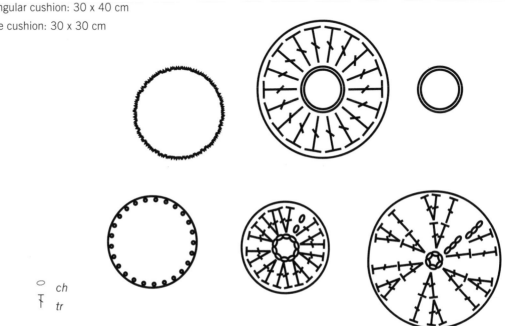

○ ch
Ŧ tr

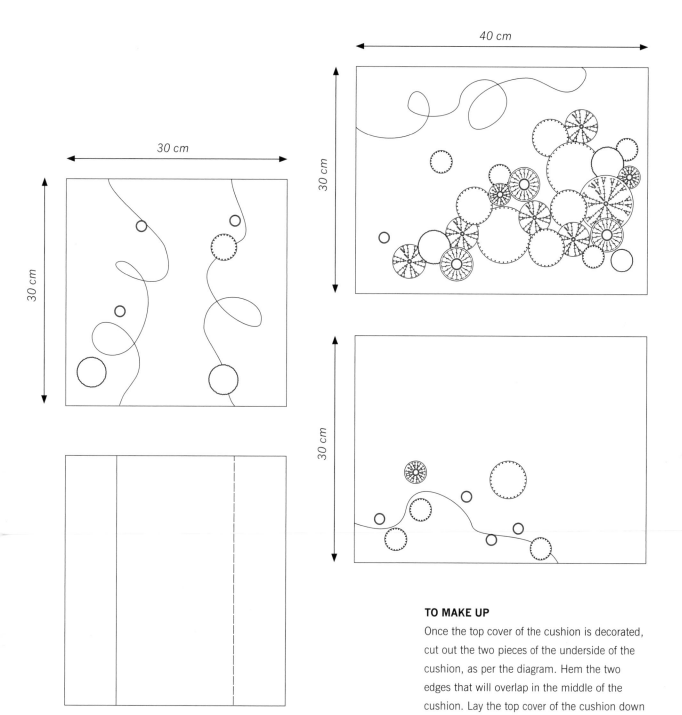

40 cm

30 cm

30 cm

30 cm

30 cm

TO MAKE UP

Once the top cover of the cushion is decorated, cut out the two pieces of the underside of the cushion, as per the diagram. Hem the two edges that will overlap in the middle of the cushion. Lay the top cover of the cushion down flat, right side upwards and place on top the two halves of the back of the cushion cover, overlapping the hemmed edges. Sew up the sides of the cushion cover, turn the piece right side out and slip the cushion inside. Sew two buttons on one half of the back of the cushion cover and make two treble stitch loops opposite them on the other half.

A big thank you to those who helped me to create this book: Doreen Harris and her knitters, Kasai, Manami Shimazaki, Doreen Payne, Kayoko Brown, Tomoko Hatano, Phyllis Van der Merwe for her embroidery; Llona Pierskalla, Alma Everritt, Catriona and James Maloney who posed for the photos; Katy Bevan for her editing, Naomi Johnstone for the technical illustrations; Koji Udo, Hiroko Mori and Kumi Saito for the beautiful photos; Doreen and Angela of Queene and Belle (www.queeneandbelle.com) for giving me permission to shoot in their Scottish studio; Tamayo Suzuki and Alison Thomas for helping me in my studio; Craig, Andre and Sabine, my sources of inspiration.

Published in 2010 by Murdoch Books Pty Limited

Murdoch Books Australia
Pier 8/9
23 Hickson Road
Millers Point NSW 2000
Phone: +61 (0) 2 8220 2000
Fax: +61 (0) 2 8220 2558
www.murdochbooks.com.au

Murdoch Books UK Limited
Erico House, 6th Floor
93–99 Upper Richmond Road
Putney, London SW15 2TG
Phone: +44 (0) 20 8785 5995
Fax: +44 (0) 20 8785 5985
www.murdochbooks.co.uk

Publisher: Kay Scarlett
Translator: Melissa McMahon
Editor: Georgina Bitcon

Text, design and illustration copyright © Marabout 2008

National Library of Australia Cataloguing-in-Publication Data

Author:	Nogichi, Hikaru.
Title:	Made in France Knitting : Baubles, scarves, cushion and more to knit and crochet / Hikaru Nogichi.
ISBN:	9781741966046 (pbk.)
Series:	Made in France.
Subjects:	Knitting. Knitting--Patterns. Crocheting. Crocheting--Patterns.
Dewey Number:	746.432041

A catalogue record for this book is available from the British Library.

PRINTED IN CHINA.